REFERENCE
≠
ENDORSEMENT

Copyright 2025 © A J Moore

ISBN: 978-1-916541-20-7

First edition.

All rights reserved.

First published in 2025 by Erratum Press
Sheffield, UK
www.erratumpress.com

Design and typesetting by Ansgar Allen

Reference ≠ endorsement of any products, companies, websites etc. namechecked in this collection.

REFERENCE
≠
ENDORSEMENT

A J Moore

ERRATUM PRESS

> Where does culture come from? It comes from
> the materials you do it with.
>
> – Alice Notley, *Culture of One*

> a cliché is not to be despised: its automatic comfort is the happy
> exteriority of a shared language which knows itself perfectly well to
> be a contentless but sociable turning outward toward the world
>
> – Denise Riley, *Impersonal Passion: Language as Affect*

> Our perception ends in objects, and the object once constituted,
> appears as the reason for all the experiences of it which we have
> had or could have.
>
> – M. Merleau-Ponty, *Phenomenology of Perception*

> These migrating objects which wash up in our homes have different histories, the consequence of the ebb and flow of daily life
> penetrating the imaginary.
>
> – Roland Topor, trans Terry Hale *Introduction II, An Anecdoted Topography of Chance by Daniel Spoerri (the edition of 1990)*

Contents

GEN/HHOLD/FOOD/1/BREAD   1
[br261121] shaping
[br011221] staff of life
[br091221] milling
[br151221] breaking bread
[br211221] rising?
[br020623] yielding
[br040122] all sorrows are less
[br060122] resting

[re 201023] **I WANNA BE LIKE YOU?**   10

GEN/HHOLD/MISC/2/CANDLES   12
[c240222] that dining out glamour
[c020322] there is romance in candle-light
[c090322] light of the world
[c080723] to cast a shadow
[c180322] at both ends
[c140423] moth to a flame
[c040422] put out the light
[c080422] brief candles

[re240223] **'NO HOPE IN DAINTINESS AND DETERMINATION'**   21

GEN/HHOLD/FURN/3/BOOKSHELVES 25
[bk210722] hers for the reading
[bk200722] primary sources
[bk290722] mis-shelving
[bk040822] co-authoring
[bk240822] third edition
[bk290822] renewing
[bk050922] remote access
[bk090922] expository texts

[re240423] **TRIPLE LETTERED ACCEPTANCE** 34

[re240423] **FOLLOWING THE RULE** 37

GEN/HHOLD/CRCK/4/PLATES 39
[p211222] what they've always wanted
[p060223] guaranteed to be perfect
[p120123] crazed
[p070223] living with style
[p170123] glazed
[p100123] to make mealtimes more fun
[p100223] shop the look
[p270123] modulus of rupture

[re181023] **KEEPING UP WITH THE JONESES?** 48

GEN/HHOLD/LNNS/5/BEDDING 51
[be090623] changing the bed
[be190623] security blanket
[be230623] clean sheet?
[be280623] uncovering
[be140723] hospital corners
[be180723] somnambulism
[be210723] safe in their beds
[be250723] re-covering

[re241023] *WHY WINNICOTT NOW?* 60

GEN/HHOLD/FURN/6/DINING TABLE 63
[dt221223] mature: fully established
[dt020124] senior
[dt110124] twilight
[dt160124] harvesting
[dt180124] sapling
[dt220124] dormant
[dt020224] late bloomer
[dt120224] veteran

[re050324] **MAKING THE BEST OF IT** 72

[re110324] **BRIDGING** 75

References and works cited 78
Notes on intertextual sources 85
Acknowledgements 91

GEN/HHOLD/FOOD/1/BREAD

[br261121] **shaping**

housekeeping won't stretch to splintered church hall's draughty weigh-ins but borrowed planner pledges spiral bound salvation [with mix 'n' match flip segments] cheerless tallied mealtimes mapped in topaz citrine blush revisiting nightly [with *Nationwide* school office drama] the edgy post mortem of *what was saved* breakfasts pack-ups bank holiday suppers evaluated benchmarked by BHS one-piece's brown floral yardstick each serenely hijacked by this incarnation's grapefruit halves fragile slices scant alpine-fresh foretastes of fibre shakes flakes whisper [re]renewed optimism light-baked strip-lit shelved between Mothers Pride® Sunblest® stale last-ditch sacrament of low-cal assurance skimmed milk tea stocked up [Thursdays] from Challenge endorsed consecrated in clipped gallant RP *don't forget* and *be smarter* and *scale down* then you too can fly [br011221] **staff of life**

steadfast sliced white anchor perennial mark of
composure and *good things* thin crust consolation
for fitful upheaval because colorectal surgeons because
Noele Gordon because General Cemetery because S11
because panic buying because neo-liberalism because
months reorienting palliative fine-milled mixed and
kneaded [with added remembrance] of jewellers of Jess
Yates of St Augustines of Dovedale of *full employment*
of post-war consensus of years prized protein-rich staple
[with added resolve] delivered [with banter] by Arthur
on Wednesdays halved spread and served [at weekends]
in the front room with saturnine gossip vicarious prayer
with hearth-softened butter beef paste sandwich filler

[br091221] **milling**

at lunchtimes a new subcollection: unrefined companion to elderly terraces *Blue Peter Swap Shop* brisk high fibre rival [brim-full of B vitamins] to *no pierced ears* Start Rite® enlarged documented in involuntary difference's over-proved cache worthy visibility's unsought distinction baked-in unbelonging untempered by overlooked Primula French Fries® clingfilm-wrapped denial of raw introversion's coveted panacea [cloned crustless moist sandwiches three-bedroomed semis *Magpie Tiswa*s gold sleepers and peep-toes from Saxone®] hungered anonymity's unscripted reminder tagged access controlled drowned out by brass bands and contagious nostalgia fragmented exported for <reading list only>

[br151221] **breaking bread**

eventual guard dropping yeast-leavened victor accepting unphased by *non-standardised south east* long-distance monogamy habitual quick-fix [with Thunderbird® Mad Dog®] of fag-smoke fogged respite from pyretic all-nighters' grade-chasing reflection and televised war [on a third-hand cracked screen] stalled third year deliverance's crisp comforting stop-gap its bite-sized amnesia from Larkin's *lonely tower* scuds and *surgical strikes* epiphanic pouches torn double-dipped bonded with darts Pictionary® with *Manhattan Cable* and Hendrix and hummus fast tenable surrogacy of unfulfilled kinship trades diligent remoteness for hair's breadth 2:i two years' hesitation for handwritten playlists evasive inclusion's slow-burn restitution *wishful sinful* quick-cooked but firm-set enduring [br211221] **rising?**

artisanal *select* extra virgin drizzled journey to waged domesticity's subconscious replica inescapable unchecked by minimal chic mortgage pressured upscaling lightly toasted disguise of inured repetition bedazzled misdirected by breezy coercive room-changing chintz-chucking ambient legerdemain of envisaged finesse *there for you*'s ignis fatuus frothy MDF constructs *lean formula* redo of chipboard and French sticks and Friday night viewing inherited custom's vicenarian rebuttal [*Cybill Frasier Friends* *blatant* on-trend distinction from *Roseanne Cheers The Golden Girls*] stained hardwood slatted blind for ordained circularity branded disowned-cemented by matte black metal candlesticks [instead of silver] by pre-weekend *humour* not post-work guffawing by sundried tomato baked brie avocado

[br020623] **yielding**

the margarine-pooled midnight supper of champions [when they finally bring something other than water] two barely-browned squares of claggy analgesia their limp antiseptic-edged shot in the arm a cardboardy lukewarm low outlay exchange for 65 hours' contraction dilation episiostomic forceps assisted yielding laceration incision unfuelled fatigue anaesthetised scorned by fentanyl-laced euphoria half-baked invincibility tight-swaddled suspended with unbending unconditional limitless love in oxytocin-and-carb loaded rhinitic unknowing of stretched processed haste's mute metabolising storm [for now] sleeping in temperate cellular softness [for now] in the untainted unaware dark this underdone over-chewed banquet will do

[br040122] **all sorrows are less**

for household use only sleek worktop placebo numbs leaden anxiety [hours owed paediatricians Gordon Brown's vacillation] hard-sold faux control's chirpy clean-eating sanction sedative slow-food surety [rye spelt and granary malted brown basic raisin] deadens holds *provides structure* to frail fractured utopia's insisting uncertainty *just mix* twice-weekly tonic of on loan stability snatched unworried nurturing pre-set relaxed raised for *warm breakfast treats* gluten dulled RHR sober self-medication's short cut rabbit's foot stirred fermented and seeded with hybrid-homegrown rite to reset restore *If baking is not complete* → *Repeat steps 1-3* [br060122] **resting**

blanket curbed interaction's curt overnight release five decades' compliance cultivated unreserve xerostomic dread the pasted-on smiles of school discos and freshers' week *meeting the parents* team-building ice-breakers stayed reprieved paroled to unleashed ISFP's still civil refusal unobtrusive demurral of bullish extroversion's bluff enforced agenda Peloton® Tik Tok *Tiger King* lower-key more avoidable than three-line-whip mingling awaydays and small talk its ersatz enthralment to foible rumour silk wraps furtive recouped control of cathartic negation unmonopolised meetings [with camera-free options] the clandestine thrill of forty minute time-outs the wilful defiance and hushed liberation of neglecting to maintain a sourdough starter

[re 201023] I WANNA BE LIKE YOU?

Clarks' closed toe sandals, BBC not ITV, atypical lunch-box contents... growing up, anything [however apparently trivial] that in any way drew attention, made me seem different from my white-bread-munching, flip-flop wearing peers was a source of [unarticulated] unrelenting unease. It is probably not news to anyone that human beings like to belong: writing in *Psychology Today* Kelly-Ann Allen notes that it has long been and continues to be 'a basic human need'.[1] But Allen also suggests that there is, in contemporary society, an argument for reframing, reconsidering notions of belonging: 'fitting in', she proposes, might be a more appropriate reflection of this need which, she reminds us, 'differs greatly among people'.[2] In my case, the drive to achieve an alternative kind of 'fitting in' lay [I realise now] not so much in a desperate yearning to follow the crowd, nor a reaction to being teased, given a hard time [I wasn't] or even particularly noticed. It was more that I wanted to be in the background. Low-profile. Wallpaper. Muzak. I liked it that way and it was crucial to me that my hiddenness was ring-fenced. Protected. Preserved.

We might contemplate that, for those of us with introverted personality types, the already manifold nature of 'fitting in' has an additional stratum of complexity, shot through, piled up, fuelled with paradox and contradiction. We are likely, as Jenn Grannemann has written, to 'feel out of place in society',[3] have a sense that we are unlike many of the people with whom we interact. Notwithstanding this out-of-step-ness, it has been widely documented that the introverted do not tend as a consequence to feel lonely or seek validation, compelled, perhaps, to 'be like' friends, loved ones, colleagues. What these 'different needs and social preferences'[4] do mean, though, is that introverted personalities often 'don't want to stand out or be noticed'.[5] All of which leaves us in somewhat of a double bind, caught between the unsettling rock of conspicuous unbelonging and compromised fitting in's dislocating hard place. It is, therefore, unsurprising to read that the Covid-19 lockdowns of 2020 and 2021 – which for many introduced the ultimate invisibility cloak of video- and audio-free work meetings – were significantly more tolerable for individuals with introverted personality types than for those who are extroverted.[6] Which is not in any way to diminish the isolation felt by millions during the pandemic, the experience of those for whom WFH was not an option or, indeed, the various coping mechanisms adopted.

We might also contemplate, then, that what may on the surface appear to indicate a wish to be like everyone else could, for the introverted personality, represent not simply materialism, social aspiration or just plain neediness [though these can, undoubtedly, be true as well – we're introverts, not saints] but something altogether more nuanced: a strategy for safeguarding our difference. Perhaps the child who craves sliced white bread and gold ear studs might, in reality, relish wholemeal sandwiches and dread the piercing gun, just as the teenager who delights in their duvet and blushes at the twin tub may have no more actual interest than their late adopter parents in state-of-the-art domestic goods. Ditto the student feeling uncomfortably marked out by their full grant, Edwardian terraced home and northern accent who hates modern houses and has no desire to 'standardise' their flat vowels. Perhaps this acute awareness of standing out speaks not to a wanting to 'fit in', but rather a needing to [as unobtrusively as possible] get on with our lives in a way that works for us. For which [at least] some kind of awkward rapprochement with the crowd could be necessary.

GEN/HHOLD/MISC/2/CANDLES

[c240222] **that dining out glamour**

but it's raining again so instead tutored housecraft rookie home economics soft cloth initiation naive satisfaction of sponging and sticking its musty-sweet clash [alkyl sulphate gum arabic] pacific sconce shining painstaking collation of Co Op and Green Shield shared ritualised primping of revered wedding gift's three branched unburned hauteur [in embossed EPNS] for *more* humble unuse improvised half-term bonding's wan silverplate stratum layered unnoted insight of 77-hour week's contact hungry routine gnawing wonted monotony foam cleansed fragmentation coated lifted infused with cathartic intrusion [Jimmy Young Maxwell House®] makeshift weekday patina on centuries' tarnish swabbed buffed up brushed out reapplying the gleam and [c020322] **there is romance in candle-light**

as stale oilclothed shelves reappraised rearranged their shoe-boxed bills bank statements streamlined demoted for prospective power shortages' resolute stockpiled saviours approved *National Wax Brand* its stacked stoic six packs [in no-nonsense white] and gathered up empties [Watneys® Woodpecker® Blue Nun®] vinegar flushed remnants of Match of the Day Sunday evening roasts repurposed on standby pre-emptive mitigation for tether's end winter's fused final straw stand starchy anxious monochrome's abrupt half-heard bulletins unheeded no match for unknowing childhood's snug pastel-dyed undisturbed winceyette dreams of smashing flame-lit larks and heart-stopping adventure [with *lashings* of silver spoon paperback promise] downsized reimagined in blanket tent dens cold beans straight from the can [c090322] **light of the world**

then the doomsday dial flashes its glacial three minute grimace-reminder unyielding omnipresent *This is the sound* backdrop to TopShop *The Tube* to double maths ceremony then implored indemnity of [fingers-crossed] *Nuclear Free Zone's* cleaved hollow defence underwritten backed up by dapper once-yearly whole-family piety then the *Little Christ Child's* foil-cloaked symbolic force field of 100% stearin dried fruits and citrus then disdained-cradled by too-visible mid-teen no-longer-believer begrudgingly forgoing top 40's uranium tainted existential crisis for single-use pseudo balm of *not walking in darkness* then sheepishly shuffling sisal-runnered aisles in weekend's full-on would-be indie kid civvies [oversized paisley beads brooches and plaits] then head bowed hedging iterating practised mental entreaties to disarm the warheads deliver a boyfriend then [c080723] **to cast a shadow**

and contoured lead crystal's simulated ice-[after]glow taunts infiltrates haunts required 4pm Chaucer [skipped last week to dodge Friday's *peak travel* fares] its reproachful ten syllable tube-lit collision of ill-prepared *Part IIs* and blister-pack quartet's [as yet unconfirmed] high stakes high dose acquittal discordant recollection of three weekly visit's luminescent reunion rough blanketed terminally beige college lodgings glimmering softened thawed by souvenir Swedish designed atmospherics slo-mo separation's heart-on-sleeve mixtapes | guttering rigid paused in fickle protection's blazing hormonal thrall [manufactured in Germany by Schering AG] to unvoiced hypervigilance stomach cramps calendars blank-eyed camouflage of flickering fluorescent sequestered focus sleepwalk marginalia stay silent in distance sneak gin into tea and murmur the fretful mailed C90 rosary: *Love me say you do*

[c180322] **at both ends**

though it's still only Thursday eleventh hour bus scraped with well-rehearsed ease transaction completed with red-eyed unquenched monosyllabic flair supported bought off by continental shifts' floating Faustian pact [rotational rest days midday starts and Sundays] hard-won first full-time contract's steady income relief from unwaged internships claims *living* back at home to novice paid weekly overdue getaway and house-share box room's twee greying net-curtained salve its in-vogue masquerade of rag rugs batik drifting rainbows of tea-lights and gemstone bright glass beads [inspired by Wax Lyrical purchased from Spoils] a wannabe boho catch-your-breath bolt-hole in work-pub-home-work's blithe circadian cycle ylang ylang scented stage set for unrealised unthinking's wax-sapping hiatus to free-form featherweight *carpe diem* myopia coasting double-burned distracted through under-read newspapers and unwatched news of exhumed interred brutality ratified persecution violation restriction

[c140423] **moth to a flame**

now cautiously anchored adjusted upgraded to tercet of svelte stemmed stylised functionality its consciously lustreless *less is more* union [modest black lacquered steel undyed paraffin wax] dialled back [not so low] budget stealth built halfway house to upward mobility's unobserved [unadmitted?] smooth slow burning draw the spun aspirational triple threat beacon [promotion home ownership co-habitation] ignited mapped out by procured understatement's soft-sold/upsold blueprint [→ cutlery → breezy linens → flat-pack storage solutions] stoked misplaced ambition's emboldening kindling its susurrate self-assembly homochrome drip to cheer-led commitment incremental conformity the smouldering sly status inflaming trinity: office-wear acquiescent *clean lines* couples' dinners

[c040422] **put out the light**

till arch lambent development stirs breaks ranks cranks up its fleet milestone-affirming jump scare two-fold ambush gleeful new-found reach of rash inquiring hands poised impatient teeth's pressing pulsing duress first time fraught fear-of-failure-fuelled accelerants for endlessly watchful fomented anxiety's lights out all-out overthought overnight clearance of pillars and multi-wicks tapers and trivets sought snuffed relocated in underused cupboards *third bedroom* oblivion wax fed avulsion of dentine and gingiva brittle doubted instinct displaced [self] maintenance stuttering perspective the *what if* inextinguishable power burn drive to monitor future-proof predict protect its skipped meal dark circled fire-fighting pursuit running to stand still stand up be *good enough* [c080422] **brief candles**

if luminous tall retreat watch at the window distrustful alert to whispered south westerly's warm-breathed deceit [hostile impulsive gusts squally underhand spray] set tenterhooks lingering the cupped-hands *strike gently* repeat re-ignition of buffeted tunnelling doorstep memorial its undaunted won't-rest-don't-give-up intensity observed witnessed photographed logged but unposted small last act of kindness collective embrace too often restated too essential stand against too commonplace too long uncounted atrocity the ingrained blame-shifting sixth sense second-guessing and ~~well-meaning~~ lip-service glib list of *don'ts* catalysed flash point fanning of synced solidarity's climate-worn flame its glinting fourteen hundred degree resolution [with posthumous gentleness] reclaimed relumed

[re240223] 'NO HOPE IN DAINTINESS AND DETERMINATION'[1]

Bored, corralled indoors on rained-off half term afternoons I would help my mother clean the silver-plated candelabra, stick customer reward scheme stamps from Mum's supermarket shop or Dad's petrol into dog-eared, jaundiced collectors' books. While it didn't compare with cycling in the park or inching round the back yard on flimsy ankle-wrenching roller skates there was a certain novelty, a satisfaction even, in seeing the shiny metal emerging radiantly from its blackened cocoon, or completing a full page – better still a whole book – of stamps. It was, it seemed, not such a bad way to spend your day.

At about the same time that these routine domestic tasks began to present [for me] an apparently acceptable ad hoc solution to my wet-weather boredom, the sociologist Ann Oakley was publishing a radical work which was to become fundamental in redefining the way housework was viewed, both within established sociological practice and by society more generally. In *The Sociology of Housework* (1974), housework is classified as actual work – rather than 'merely as an aspect of the feminine role in the family'[2] – and, furthermore, revealed to be a source of boredom and isolation: feelings of 'fragmentation', 'monotony' and 'loneliness'[3] were commonplace for the women Oakley interviewed. It is only recently that I have paused to consider that maybe the ubiquitous presence of the radio in various of my family's homes [BBC Radio 2 for Mum, BBC Radio Sheffield for my Grandma and 'The Third Programme' for my Nan] might have represented something other than simply a love of music.

Oakley's study also highlighted the punishing nature of the weekly working hours for her respondents, which for most totalled 'between seventy and eighty-nine'[4] – way in excess of the commitment expected of those in full time paid employment. Additionally, Oakley invites the reader to reflect on the role of media messaging and the matrilineal handing on and 'rehearsal' of domestic tasks in creating a sense of 'obligation' [I don't recall the carefully sponged and buffed candelabra ever being used], a need to replicate 'previously set standards' which, in reality, are impossible to consistently maintain.[5] Think Fairy Liquid's series of commercials from the 1960s and 1970s in which a mother assiduously describes its superior dish-cleaning properties to a female child while simultaneously reassuring her that it will keep her hands soft over the day's many washes. Regardless of how consciously [or not] this handing on takes place, it is certainly hard to believe that my grandmother, having no daughters, would have encouraged my father to while away a few damp hours by bleaching the toilet or ironing some sheets.

Over half a century before Oakley finally made explicit the unspun, unglossed reality of these women's experience, the experimental examination of household objects in Gertrude Stein's *Tender Buttons* (1914) feels remarkably prescient of her findings. If we read Stein's 1910s poems with Oakley's 1970s research in mind we might see, perhaps, in the fragmented text and syntactic disruptions a foreshadowing of the fragmented nature of housework described by Oakley's participants. We might also find a synergy between repeated words and motifs both within Stein's individual poems and across the collection – 'dirt', dustiness, cleanliness, a sense of what is 'necessary' – and the concerns raised by Oakley's interviewees when recounting the pressures they feel. One such repetition – 'disgrace' – may be said to go even further, its use in conjunction with objects so intensely associated with perceptions of femaleness reinforcing notions that a lack of attention to cleanliness – either in the home or in connection with sexual purity – is an undesirable trait in a woman and, moreover, something by which she is judged.[6] Based on this comparison it seems, despite a sixty year gap and many societal changes between the two publications, both Stein and Oakley are signposting that the female sense of self *and* the way that self is viewed by society are inextricably bound up with the ability to satisfactorily execute housework tasks.[7]

A further half century on from Oakley's study, then, does it still have resonances in twenty first century Britain? We would probably all agree that, with increased numbers of women entering the workplace in the intervening fifty years, the allocation of domestic duties has necessarily evolved, changed for the better. However, research undertaken throughout this period suggests there is still some distance to go. In the 1990s, for example, Duncombe and Marsden found that, as a result of these changes, women were now working a 'triple shift', which involved paid employment, housework and taking on the bulk of the 'emotion work' required to sustain relationships with partners and family.[8] More recently, a 2016 survey by the Office of National Statistics disclosed that, on average, women were doing 40% more of household chores and childcare than men.[9] Meanwhile, a project by the Institute of Fiscal Studies and University College London revealed that during the Covid-19 lockdown of 2020, this situation was exacerbated, meaning 'in homes where there is a working mother and father,[10] women are doing more chores and spending more time with children'.[11] In terms of how this is reflected in the media, we might again consider Fairy, whose commercials for dishwasher tablets feature [at time of writing] a gruff voiced cartoon biker baby paired with a female voice-over [though their laundry products, despite now focussing on health and safety, still depict a mother and child scenario]. And ultimately, despite being eased by an ever-increasing arsenal of hi-tech gadgets housework remains – for me and for many others, I'm sure – boring, unrewarding, unrewarded. So, what exactly is it that keeps us bought in, locked in never-ending rubber-gloved combat with self-propagating cat fluff, toast crumbs, coffee grounds? Among the untarnished memories of those rainy afternoons, do the legacy of 'obligation', the fear of 'disgrace' still loiter, sleeves rolled up, cloth in hand?

GEN/HHOLD/FURN/3/BOOKSHELVES

For Anne Armitage (1916-2003)

[bk210722] hers for the reading

of pre-Butler exclusion's retrospective soft-cover DIY education double-stacked library surplus from Collins and Gollancz the fag-melted dust-bloomed clear laminate refuge of Christie and Allingham Sayers and Marsh their easy uncatalogued proud co-existence with OU natural history *Say it in Russian* treasured disparate gifts from adoring godchildren [a perpetual calendar stranded in May unremarkable pieces of beach-scavenged rock] on patched up re-revarnished mass-produced oak ingested devoured in insomniac down-time from caregiving homemaking swing shifts at Batchelors stalwart cut-price custodian of armchair polymath's hands-bound boundless third-hand holdings self-homeschooled desire the unceasing *life's what you make it* lifelong appetite refusal of bitterness unread ambition [bk200722] **primary sources**

of home-made reflexive within-means adjustments to overstuffed magazine-rack sovereignty [*Living Reader's Digest* *The Star* *The Express*] for head-over-heels fallen hard perfect bound annex *come in handy* chipboard's glossed can-end caress of caves codes and caravans islands kidnapped scientists the apple pie *ripping times* *seen on tv* hijinks their multi-million-selling quixotic allure unblemished foreshadowing of artless unquestioning teenage progression to SMERSH Soviets SPECTRE monomaniac masterminds compliant *girls* the relentless male gaze *shaken not stirred* machismo consumed ordered displayed [with Dewey Decimal pride] on redeployed brackets thrown-out-door mahogany [bk290722] **mis-shelving**

of Pope and Defoe next to Kesey O'Neill Penguin Classics [from Blackwell's] with BOGOFs from The Works Part I keystone set text scrubbed-brick-bookended signifiers' unreferenced insinuated misfiling of single waged basic rate queued for full grant among higher rate unsubsidised parental support muffled old-hand quotidian mid-terrace closeness with clearly enunciated short-let sixty week novelty the *last-in* obliged diffident people pleasing reclassified stored in unencumbered belonging's in-crowd self-assured vault [with the staunch large print nag of unfavourable remembering] dust jacketless indexed on permanent loan [bk040822] **co-authoring**

of fixed rate allegiance's double-signed lender approved collaboration guaranteed interest first draft of cross-genre connectivity *other halves'* guilty pleasures' coy tentative blending space opera cyberpunk alternate history reshuffled bedfellows to Rebus and Morse categorised alphabetised on veneered low-sheen flat pack particleboard [*inspired by traditional carpentry*] the off the peg effortless tongue-and-groove lure of happy ever after's must-have *urban lifestyle* its uncluttered unadorned understated demand to re-order rationalise take a risk on twenty five year plan permanence forever fidelity the will-writing cat-owning joint bank account push to rehome twice-bought Bowie and duplicate Dickens [bk240822] **third edition**

of irretrievably fading friable memento's precarious bowed limb flaking finish refuge for handed down Hill cracked-spine donated Dexter unable to withstand another house move succeeded [not replaced] by Scandi-aspirant *Modular Tall Shelf Unit* [*90 minutes approximately 2 people assembly*] its *classic oak effect ample storage* cradling of newly-discovered spiralling Nordic noir [Mankell and Indridason Sjöwall and Wahlöö] reassigned [not demoted] as pre-weathered framework for ad libbed raised bed reallocated nourishment of [uninvited] blackberries wild strawberries mint recollecting retracing ineradicable darkening make-do-and-mend footsteps their conjured peach stone grown Carnation® slicked fruit Sellotape® anchored carpet squares and snapped windscreen wipers an edgeworn Pan reprint of *4.50 From Paddington*

[bk290822] **renewing**

of cubic plate glass screened *second time around* coupling courted clinched consummated with post-war modernist Grade II listed come-on from uptight out of form breathy tentative fumblings in back-to-back humid multilevel racks to dry-mouthed anticipation of steel-framed seduction unshelved BA (Hons) quarter century tradition's awakened unstructuring pursued smooth-talked teased in beat-skippingly brazen *next-level* encounters on chapbook strewn broadside spattered reading room desks the limited print run letterpress kissed path to uncontainable union boundary pushing relief impetuous closed stack *by appointment* abandon [bk050922] **remote access**

of *too little too late too flawed* forcible parting *forewarned but not forearmed* hedged procrastinated passage to borderless LDR's needy pre-filtered congress *anywhere in the record* on virtual shelves [sporting bobbled pyjamas ghd® rebuffed hair] its hands-off TMC *strategic relation maintenance* [accessed 27 March 2020] through ProQuest Ebook Central tandfonline JSTOR vicarious intimacy of SED digitised interlibrary loans' untouchable surrogate *hungered for touch* searched stock-checked requested [by keyed in live chat] for copyright-friendly single download succour emailed affirmation [accessed… accessed… accessed…]

[bk090922] **expository texts**

of delegated establishment bibliophile clout's tiered *zoom room* disclosed pre-pandemic facades curated convened by tight-lipped connoisseurs for on-brand agenda-led movers and shakers tactically literary 'A' list celebs or remaindered set-dressing bulk-bought by the yard selected staged Fed-Exed to hotels home offices steroid pumped boardrooms or coplanar gold-tooled textured calfskin *tomes* reproduced on collapsible phthalate-free vinyl despatched [FOC] within three working days or synthetically eclectic travelogues Greek tragedy weird fiction on *timelessly elegant* wax finished pine colour-sorted imported to Skype Google Meet or forlorn hasty assemblage of PPE textbooks arbitrary biographies scavenged dug out by aides perfunctorily columned under Twitterstorm's Fresnel lensed foreground-lit glare cut-rate hardback diplomacy hacked credibility custom-built shipped steam-ironed uploaded laid bare

[re240423] TRIPLE LETTERED ACCEPTANCE

Go-to autological abbreviated patch for time-poor restricted-character based communication, the TLA [Three Letter Acronym] saturates our contemporary linguistic interactions, from business meetings and scientific documents to song lyrics and social media posts. It's even a pin-up for its own condensed cleverness, its USP being the fact that it makes use of its basic principles to describe itself. That has to be a good thing, right? Well, maybe if you're one of those "in the know", whose inside track intelligence allows them to decode, process, understand [which would itself make quite a neat TLA, but a quick survey of the multiple acronym finders available online doesn't appear to list this as one of the many possible meanings of DPU] the message being relayed. We should also consider that the sense of satisfaction we can [probably] assume this creates for the decoder likely does not end there, but rather – in common with accents, dinner plates and your sandwich loaf of choice – makes such [apparently] practical, accessible shorthand another means of expressing belonging to a particular group,[1] a truncated passport to clued up fitting in. In which case, we might equally consider, as Eryc Eyl has discussed, that it will as well have the capacity to be a means of keeping out. For those in the uncondensed dark, the TLA all too easily becomes self-satisfied jargon, at best frustrating or embarrassing [the well-worn example of the widespread misuse of LOL springs to mind] and at worst – whether intentional or not – alienating and exclusionary. In this collection, you will find TLAs – many of them unfamiliar to the general reader – drawn from a miscellaneous assortment of sources, including popular brands, building materials, medical terminology, text/online lexis, information technology, commerce and finance. Why did I use them? IDK, maybe I was attempting to make some enciphered point about language as a mechanism for control but, TBH, sometimes they just scan better.

Glossary of TLAs

BHS	British Home Stores (p. 2)
MDF	Medium-density fibreboard (p. 6)
RHR	Resting heart rate (p. 8)
BBC	British Broadcasting Corporation (pp. 10, 21, 48, 79, 81, 82)
ITV	Independent Television (p. 10)
WFH	Working From Home (p. 11)
DIY	Do-it-yourself (p. 26)
LDR	Long distance relationship (p. 32)
TMC	Technologically-mediated communication (p. 32)
SED	Secure electronic delivery (p. 32)
FOC	Free of charge (p. 33)
PPE	Politics, Philosophy and Economics (p. 33). Degree often taken in the UK by those who pursue careers in government, not to be confused with Personal Protective Equipment, the dubious procurement of which during the Covid-19 Pandemic may or may not have been influenced by alumni of such courses.
USP	Unique selling proposition (p. 34)
DPU	Options include, but are not limited to, Data Processing Unit, Development Planning Unit, Digital Processing Unit, Display Processor Unit, Delayed Pressure Urticaria (p. 34)
LOL	Laugh out loud (p. 34)
IDK	I don't know (p. 34)
TBH	To be honest (p. 35)
LTV	Loan-to-value (ratio) (p. 43)
PVO	Positive vibes only (p. 44)
VCR	Videocassette recorder (p. 54)
TPI	Threads per inch (p. 57)
CTA	Call to action (p. 58)
VHS	Video home system (p. 71)

[re240423] FOLLOWING THE RULE

Sometime during the drafting of the first sequence [Bread] in this collection, I began to notice a tendency to gather, group, collect words or phrases in threes. So much has been written about the rule of three [or triad,[1] hendiatris,[2] tricolon[3]], its capacity to make our words more memorable, impactful, aurally appealing. From literary criticism to marketing theory to the innumerable online creative writing websites, blogs, resources, the rule of three is widely documented as an attractive, effective way of capturing an audience's interest, and there seems little merit in repeating this again in any detail here. But I am curious to reflect on why this particular device seemed so eager, demanding, insistent on making its presence felt [some might argue excessively so] in the poems. I didn't consciously set out to recursively circle back to it in a deliberate attempt to arrest, engage, entertain, any more than I planned to adopt a constraint of eight poems per sequence [which, incidentally, has nothing to do with potential impact and everything to do with the number of ideas I had for the first couple of sequences, and thereafter appears to have become a something of a tradition].[4] Although – as with the rule of three abiding TLA – when something is so extensively applied we might consider that the unplanned and organic will probably give way to the calculated and deliberately constructed at some point along the road.

Perhaps the simplest explanation for our fascination with all things threefold lies in the abundance of opportunities we have to encounter it while going about our everyday business – advertising slogans, political speeches, jokes, presentations and children's literature being just a few examples. By virtue of being all around us all the time, the rule of three becomes embedded in our subconscious, so much so that 'we use it without giving it a second thought'.[5] A more scientific interpretation, meanwhile, would favour the human brain's inbuilt inclination to look for patterns, the ability to identify them having been integral to improving survival prospects for early civilisations.[6] If, as Jan Fields has remarked, the number three is, 'the smallest number of things that form a recognizable pattern' then we might assume that makes the rule of three a winning option for both its originator and its audience, being 'easily consumable' yet, at the same time, feeling 'weighty enough to be important'.[7] In these poems, I also suspect that it is a case of the [ex]-copywriter's favourite child[8] commanding attention and old habits die hard. Which, come to think of it, might also account for their [ie the poems'] predisposition to not exceed a 140 word count.

But whatever the reason [in reality, probably a combination of all the above], words seemed somehow to naturally present themselves in trinities, triumvirates, trios and I kind of got to like their addictive tripartite rhythms. For some, this undoubtedly will feel over-used, overstated, too much and I offer in mitigation the following from artist Tess Jaray:

> 'I see pattern as seeing the expression of certain kinds of order that reflect both what is in the world, and what is in oneself. There is a pattern in everything, in a sense, and of course the repetition of anything creates pattern. Some see it as being formalistic, I don't. Our lives are patterned, our lives are framed'.[9]

And will leave it there for the reader to ponder, mull over, decide.

GEN/HHOLD/CRCK/4/PLATES

[p211222] **what they've always wanted**

the swallowed discourse of oven-to-table desire line's *low residue* days wiped down *measured out* in milky white high thermal shock resistant glassware its five-two rotational seared tally marks [roses Monday – Friday blue stars for the weekends] patterned opalescent bearers of fried eggs onion gravy aureolin custard's congealed held-tongue skin on reheated ennui home-cooked quarantine rebranded burned into painted obligation of Number 10's homilies airbrushed double-spreads touting *superior quality* and talked up time saving easy care immobility so practical affordable *beautifully long-lasting*

[p060223] guaranteed to be perfect

the must-have vitrified *semi-porcelain* silence of reshaped repackaged replenished reprise its honey-voiced 36-piece clean plate covenant acquired ad hoc in side-work financed quotas from Argos new decade's new start new line same-old-shit smokescreen [ushered in with lasagne spag bol test-run chilli] for collectable co-ordinated conversationless grind passed off reinforced with auto-tuned purring primetime doublespeak coiffured cod commonality pussy-bow gilded tyranny *unseemly* objection suffocated restrained with slashed recommended retail price sweet nothings [hand-finished wildflowers a lovers' knot ribbon] an *iconic classic* and all-time best-seller [p120123] **crazed**

the silica sealed self-selected unsaying deflected decal fired with pre-Xmas scuffed home-from-home Xmas lunch [chicken microwaved veg on mismatched *slight seconds*] pissed postprandial bonding watching [rented] Bond jaunty overcorrection's bargain basement front for styled out stifled lateness's equivocating hairline cracked labyrinth [abdominal discomfort weight gain nausea] surreptitious excoriation radar evading scanning for thirsted dysmenorrhea's overdue flood lipsticked shrugged off unsatisfactorily numbed by the undigested stodge of a *licence revoked* tepid Liebfraumilch in a *value pack* tumbler

[p070223] living with style

the massed mid-price rustic stoneware breadcrumb trail to white collar nirvana salaried restratification arm's-length *old money's* petitioned place setting parboiled thin-ice admittance its just-stomached maximum LTV parity cosy misconstrued vining-rose-and-leaf vocality ravenous double-oven fired infatuation satisfied [temporarily] at appropriate intervals with kept up minutiae accessorised regard [spoon rest? tea bag tidy? 9-inch fluted flan dish?] the acquisitive overcooked *done thing* autocracy of 24/7 alta voce validation to suits seasonal gatherings outstepped shop floor friends dodged refiled as acquaintances *but chiefly* to one's selves [p170123] **glazed**

the slender resilience of slip-trailed cured surfaces formerly feared watch and wait worst-case-scenario's caught unawares *ticking clock* triggered volte face to tearing internalised pathological *want* its speculum probed fluoroscopied game face re-toughened zhuzhed up for annual down-tools non-elective indulgence mandatory festivity garnished zigzagged onto hand-thrown earth toned earthenware terracotta and burgundy PVO pandering and modestly risqué over-rehearsed yarns sunshiny unwelcome-welcome overtalking of impenetrable sloughed lining regularity aching under the table max-absorbency withholding [p100123] **to make mealtimes more fun**

the melamine easy grip amplification of saccharine-dusted gatecrasher *suggestions* signalled [sparingly] before 12-week scan before birth before solids then declared volumised with breast and not bottle and baby-led weaning for gloves-off all bets off tart unfiltered glut of *well-intentioned* pass-agg second helpings reboiled dished out in defrosted batch-cooked portion controlled instalments dysphagic unjollied by Thomas's chatty upbeat teatime primaries / unsoothed by Humphrey's subdued breakfast set pastels *at home or on the go* unshakable durable ideal to help minimise stress at the table [p100223] **shop the look**

the sterile reminiscence is moulded re-presented in analgesic *retro style* terre verde standardware for fine dining Sunday supplement *your way* re-collection of tan-and-taupe cottage pie unexceptionality treadmill low key cloth-cutting misremembered cool fetishised throwback flatware comforter's blocky geometric leaf cross-decade distraction from unfashionably premium res similarity [snap elections terror alerts economic unease] downsampled sifted hoodwinked by ecru colourways' op-ed propped skeuomorph [*you might also need* rosy-lensed *infotainment*] click here to check *your item is still an option*

[p270123] modulus of rupture

the publicity-shy gold-leafed subsidised disjunct portcullis stamped shushing of *prime* chargrilled ribeye terrines panna cotta Members-only marked down silver service estrangement discounted untroubling of *underfunded* [£84k p. a. + expenses] balance sheet the state liveried run-at-a-loss overglazing for under-researched pre-prepared pigeon-holing and rent-a-quote clickbait *from scratch* moralising its dyed-in-the-wool damask carved panelled diversions a choice of eight hand-picked speciality teas a portrait in oils by Sir Joshua Reynolds

[re181023] KEEPING UP WITH THE JONESES?

idiom: to show that one is as good as other people by getting what they have and doing what they do[1]

Every generation could probably pinpoint its own example of the stereotypically acquisitive [often female] social climbing snob beloved of satire and situation comedy, for whom ownership of, say, a certain brand of furniture a or a particular pattern of crockery is essential in demonstrating their social standing – not just to the proverbial 'Joneses' of the title but, perhaps more importantly, to themselves.[2] For me [official category: Generation X[3]] and my contemporaries, it was the BBC TV sitcom characters Margo Leadbetter,[4] and later Hyacinth Bucket[5], who became synonymous with middle class affectation and ambition, their RP enunciated Conservative Club pretensions exposed, punctured, lampooned in cosy *most watched* half hourly primetime segments. Characters that chime so resonantly with the viewer because, as Charlotte McDougall has written, 'We've all met a Margo'.[6]

On screen during a period when our parents and their peers [official category: 'Baby Boomers'[7]] would have likely been at their home-purchasing household-item-acquiring peak, we might contemplate whether these [apparently] larger-than-life fictional creations were also recognisable, replicated in the real-life behaviours of both generations. A study for the *Cultures of Consumption* project by Rebecca Leach et al (2005-2007) identified the Boomers' habit of 'Funding home extensions, conservatories, shower rooms, new bedrooms... Improving the 'value' of homes' in order 'to fund consumption in retirement'.[8] Even if not knowingly undertaken to impress the Joneses, a tendency to stretch oneself to the limit was probably viewed [both internally and externally] as evidence of fitting in, of a double-mortgaged right to a place at aspiration's extendable table [with complementary accessories]. A four-bedroom two toilet maxed-out-AmEx existence co-ordinated to within an inch of its corner-to-corner carpeted life. This Gen-Xer [somewhat self-righteously] vowed never to scramble for such procured 'matchy matchy'[9] prestige.

My vow would seem [on the face of it] to be in line with a trend which emerged in the mid-1990s–mid 2000s, the years during which many Gen-Xers would have begun making the bulk of their own property-related purchases. This era was characterised, as research by D Jasun Carr et al has pointed out, by a shift in focus from the consumption of goods in order to signify belonging to a particular group or strata to buying patterns which reflected 'your individuality, your personal sense of taste and distinction'[10] [for me, suns, moons and stars *boho chic* giving way to mock mid-mod clean lines, once-despised childhood palettes of ochre, avocado]. So far, so *unique*.[11] However, given that the period also saw a significant upturn in 'lifestyle' based popular cultural content [Sunday supplement features, the growth of celebrity brands, home improvement shows such as *Changing Rooms*][12] we might consider that we [especially the new Gen X consumers] were arguably equally in thrall to commodity-based snobbery of another kind – one whose desire for individuality extends only so far as being 'different in the right way',[13] the outcome of which may well be a homogeneity, a sort of aesthetic groupthink. Something which, it would appear, shows no signs of abating in the 2020s, with their programmes dedicated to *spaces*, *locations*, *designs*. Their weekend magazine spreads of products which one can safely assume to be way beyond the budget of most of their readership. Their stretching the concept of the celebrity brand to include the offerings of reality show contestants and social media influencers. In its own way this speaks – if not to a keeping up – then at least to a kinship with the Joneses which no amount of Scandi-inspired minimalism, tranquil neutrals and selective self-knowledge can gloss over. Perhaps, as Charlotte McDougall has suggested, 'There's a teeny bit of Margo'[14] in more of us than would care to admit it.

GEN/HHOLD/LNNS/5/BEDDING

[be090623] **changing the bed**

rumpled unspoken grief is folded down tucked into self-striped magenta and tangerine pockets of expected *keep calm and carry on* cheer tearless chin-up re-covering of [not quite] forty years' oak framed unruffled sharing with unilateral bedded in no-frills forbearance technicolored [but low maintenance] un-complaint customary [but newly lone] sleepless detecting with Marple and Campion Wimsey Alleyn shouldered smoothed out bolstered by laid-back half term ~~childcare~~ sleepovers sanguine pyjama-ed sidekicks propped Morecambe-and-Wise-like with *A Murder is Announced* and *Twinkle* [for girls] in bookish camaraderie's loud brushed nylon cocoon its *characteristically soft* sturdy touch unwrinkles unburdens *holds up very well*

[be190623] security blanket

ensconced close the door on re-layered intervention's taut overstarched wrapping of referrals -oscopies -ectomies -plasties ready restless mortality's piled-on month-on-month crumpling flattened overspread with once-a-week celadon candlewicked stasis its unslept uncreased tufted leafy repose religiously shaken out fluffed up re-straightened [with consoling drill's week-on-week slowing fingers] in solemnised industry soft fringed observance for ironed-in resignation's crisp hermetic haven its anamnestic cradling of Pledge®-heavy air freehold accommodation of memory's guests ~~anticipated~~ hypothetical ~~sleepovers~~ childcare

[be230623] clean sheet?

craved homogeneity's airy *stuffed cover* prospect untucking turning back head down polyester and flannel divergence unrolled warily draped between compromise phone [ ] ceded VCR on unfussed mid-life *laggards'* blissfully off-message off-the-pace continuum box-fresh 10.5 tog *fashion print* fitting in [with moderate fill power's trapped in bravado] peer-certified plumped up [partial] insulation against 3 tog teen sensibility's winter-weight diffidence co-opted *last 16 per cent* king size *lack* *wicking away* self-conscious self-imposed side-lining twin-tub washed immersion-heated standing out

[be280623] **uncovering**

unpracticed [almost] accidental unfolding of long awaited waited out coalescence in laundry-marked cotton uniform counterpane procrastination's overwashed scratchy mantle disentangled thrown off with unswaddled hesitancy's unloosed unminding of competence *stage fright* inadequate heating its extraordinary false start littered shift soundtracked underscored offset with minor key Saturday ordinariness [mid-morning radio's ~~zany~~ predictable repartee football studs' clacking echoey corridor hum] for blanketed sureness's unanalysed uncomplicated uncovering embedded connection bold intimacy [be140723] **hospital corners**

pulled tight close the door on on-trial *suitability's* skittish shoes-off slaloming through pressed lace-trimmed pitfalls soft-furnished scrutiny awakening tripping stiff valanced surveillance of walk-through *fourth bedroom's* offshot sleepless airlock curfewed cornered eavesdropping smothered stage whispers' [imagined?] appraisal edge under shrink down beneath pitiless plain dye double-tucked cotton a remade reorganised topsheeted self hemmed diagonally secured to *achieve the desired tension* [be180723] **somnambulism**

swayed seduced say *hej* to protested positioning's lengthened softest touch strides towards settling down's covert [caught napping] buy-in its upscaled TPI *statement* stepping stone on *immersive buying's* slumbering one-way route from toe-dipping flirtations with throws framed posters woodstain to unbridled first time joint purchased surrender to futons shaker cabinets *sofas* [not settees] through denied convention's *dreamy* night on night enveloping in breathable block striped *bed linen* [not bedclothes] [be210723] **safe in their beds**

overwhelmed thrown sink back into *oatmeal* and *magic mint* dappled confusion of counselled preparation's *delicate* overload *receiving blankets comforters sleep accessories* *adorably* heaped tangled in pitched uncrumpled idyll's guilt-crocheted layette the *super-soft* clamour of recommendations reviews ~~essential~~ indistinguishable plusses tenderly laid down snuggled in *soothing* desaturated pointelle chenille crooned CTA lullaby for **don't mess up's** implied fractious wakeful blooming so all's *right* safe and calm [today] wish list → checkout → sold ★★★★★ *exactly what we needed* [be250723] **re-covering**

bagged up relegated to spidery mildewed junk cupboard jostling with ill-thought-out curtains impulse-bought tablecloths the overconsumed emulsion-flecked debris of cyclical taste's on/off in/out dalliances [*think* *new england* foliage buffalo checks] patient jilted keepers of re-covered re-coloured autobiographies [*think* indulgent *lime* emergent *saffron* sleep deprived *light taupe*] dictated ghost-written in pilled bundled cast-offs' droplet coded folds rolled out revised rolled up interstitial waiting

[re241023] *WHY WINNICOTT NOW?*[1]

We probably have more information than ever about childrearing and parenting at our disposal, with pastel-tinted rabbit holes of advice websites, online forums, apps all pulling at our virtual sleeves, competing – like rival siblings – for our weary attention. Why, then, as Maggie Nelson reflects in *The Argonauts*, has there been a contemporary resurgence in popularity of paediatrician and psychologist D W Winnicott's mid twentieth century concept of the 'good enough mother'? Rejecting received practices of telling parents what to do in favour of the notion that 'the mother herself is the specialist in her own baby'[2] and should be allowed to trust her instincts, this revolutionary approach was, as Robert Adès has observed, 'intended to liberate parents [Winnicott has pointed out that 'good-enough mothering... includes fathers'][3] from the millstone of aspirational perfection'.[4] While we might easily imagine the parents of Winnicott's post-war Britain, still heavily influenced by 'state propaganda'[5] about health and child-rearing, overpowered, weighed down by talked-down-to stiff-upper-lipped starchy ideals, why is it that the [in theory] more compassionate 2010s and 2020s – where we are constantly promised that it's ok not to be ok – don't seem to offer the same level of assurance that it's also good enough for our parenting to be 'good enough'?

The answer to these questions might, perhaps, lie in a suspicion that the [apparently not so] analogue spirit of 'aspirational perfection' past could, in fact, be alive and well and living rent free among the helpful posts, honest blogs, adorable shares which permeate, direct our digital interactions. Health website *Patient* highlights in particular the impact of social media platforms where 'More often than not, we only see a carefully curated version of someone's life... filled with images of happy, smiling new parents who don't seem to be struggling'.[6] The execution may be more informal, but we might contemplate that the outcome could arguably be just as inhibiting as that of the overt paternalism which Winnicott sought to challenge. [Aside: a whole other commentary could be written about the earning potential these ubiquitous rose-tinted family scenarios afford to social media influencers paid to promote baby products, where consumption may well as much indicate a desire to conform to constructed beliefs about what *good* parents look like as what is simply practical or necessary – but that's for a separate interrogation]. All of which means we should maybe not be surprised to learn that a 2021 survey of new parents by children's brand Stokke found that almost a quarter of respondents 'worried about being labelled a bad parent' and felt pressure to be perfect, with '71% of mums' [as opposed to 57% of dads] admitting 'to feeling guilty for not doing or not being able to do something advised by parenting experts' and a further 81% of women experiencing guilt over their 'parenting style/choices'.[7]

The Stokke survey also namechecks that notoriously timeless source of parental anxiety unsolicited advice, which ranks fifth in its top ten list of the frustrations articulated. From sleeping positions and feeding choices to dealing with tantrums and how long to ignore crying, as soon as you have a child it can seem that everyone you meet – friends, family, casual bystanders, the guy in the corner shop – is an expert, with opinions [however well-intentioned] which they ~~offer~~ impose without stopping to consider whether they have been requested or are even welcome. My own top ten included [but was not limited to] an abundance of 'feedback' on nutrition, most notably highly personal comments concerning breastfeeding and an [apparently] genial berating over the use of shop bought jars of baby food, dispensed as carelessly as small talk about the weather or what was on the telly last night. [Aside: Winnicott was, as Adès notes, resistant 'to giving practical advice which inevitably becomes faddish over time'].[8] And while all of this can be tempered by remembering that the inclination to give unsolicited advice generally, as has been widely written on, says far more about the adviser's need for control than the advisee's need for guidance, this is not something which necessarily springs easily to mind when sleep deprived and finding one's way through a significant life-changing event.

Exposed 24/7 to such constant and increasing pressures, the new [and not so new] parenting self must, surely, be up there as one of the most scrutinised identities of all. In *The Argonauts*, Maggie Nelson expresses the following wish for her unborn child:

> Let him stay oblivious – for the first and last time, perhaps – to the task of performing a self for others, to the fact that we develop, even in utero, in response to a flow of projections and reflections ricocheting off us.[9]

Time to reclaim being 'good enough'.

GEN/HHOLD/FURN/6/DINING TABLE

[dt221223] **mature: fully established**

extendable drop-leafed gate-legged centrepiece to buckled *Dunkirk spirit's* regathered derationed secured loan deferral re-rooted beginnings still healthy *still spreading* with *looking up's* glossy [so far] unsapped vigour through unrested rest day's piled-up finger buffets their ox tongue and piccalilli Sunday night payback for 6-day week 40-a-day flat out graft an [assumed] evergreen bread-and-butter upholding of Lyons loose leaf earnest collar-and-tie chat budding blossoming into unwound shirt-sleeved sideshoots [sweet sherry brown ale *Doll Dance* banged out by ear] undented absorbing the knocks *built to last* [dt020124] **senior**

recommissioned reopened oak-clad amnesty from cramped kitchen formica's day on day decline polished dressed reinstated [for one restaged night only] to once-weekly heyday's unstiffened full-stretch groaning overladen with dignity's transposed Boxing Day re-enactment of yesterday's steamed-up overdone excess hardwired hospitality's heavier limbed comeback in retrenched proof of life's festive familiar *short sprouts* [sports jackets and frocks roast capon *Don Cortez*] unbowed keeping their end up *for just one more year* its white-clothed resurrection effortful sustaining [dt110124] **twilight**

collapsed stashed away behind aluminium and polypropylene trespass of reconfigured living's overfilled microcosm blanked undusted shrinking among snagged rasped out twilight's metastatic clutter [commode walking frame *carers height* single bed] until pressed into hastily sterilised service for individual servings of post-discharge platters [leg drainage bags kidney bowls latex free gloves] their unboxed nested takeover halted refused by unseen plastic chrysanthemums' edged out resistance *useful life's* *tiny twigs* in a cream SylvaC vase

[dt160124] harvesting

earmarked claimed uprooted at stonewalled postwake walk-through's queasy damp-palmed in-and-out pre-clearance sweep round the standard lamps side tables powder bowls doilies of archived matrimony's untouched unaired tableaux to join harvested chosen ones' smug side door clique the uncredited back-of-the chorus-line cousin of jazz hands collectible Singer and Ferguson wrangled lugged transplanted to indefinite cobwebbed dust-sheeted suspension an attic room seed bed for [re]germination [dt180124] **sapling**

rediscovered removed to a *permanent* [?] *spot* a lead comeback role in chanced unfurnished joining's magpied kitting out stable trusted kernel to faceless furnished rentals' pooled unconstant blooms [oil burners cd towers rattan plant stands] one leaf down re-rooted with second-hand settled-for fixtures and fittings [an immovable wardrobe a grumbling fridge] for *just begun's* flexible unripened hosting with Delia *Good Food Entertaining With Cranks* [dt220124] **dormant**

both leaves down to move over stand in the wings for first-hand refurnishing's first anniversary debut [in toughened glass wrought iron and pu leather] an off-the-peg trouper death-masked understudy to bespoke newcomer's polished scene-stealing its diva-ish need to be de-smudged dressed set fallow woodenly safeguarding unbinned placeless relics [coupons takeaway menus the *good* birthday cards] hibernating purpose's unbowed cambium keeping on still word perfect *ready to pop*

[dt020224] **late bloomer**

pulled out cast against type in *fully operational* pandemic two-hander with *distinguished* principal's spiffy aging swagger [VG showing *some signs of cosmetic wear*] a socially distanced pared-back one-act re-staging [with cut short present-swapping two-course plated-up meal] unevenly costumed in poinsettia red and sateen snowflake print its wintering fitness re-nourished reaching warmed by untested shared credit's known strengthening props clustered votives crowded pans an over-worked fan oven [dt120224] **veteran**

re-folded recast a backstage habitat pitted scarred *vital shelter* for theirs-hers-his medley of unhomed wanted outliers rootless *square pegs* [VHS tapes hot water bottle a *co-operative board game*] their affable dissonance tended upheld by a hewn second life poised to outlast its first homeware ecosystem's steadying *slow dying* cover hanging tight holding out for one last featured part a seasoned *old stager* unbroken survivor cued up to be called back revived handed on [?]

[re050324] MAKING THE BEST OF IT[1]

Women are 'socalized to be nice from a very young age, encouraged to ignore our own needs and put those of others first',[2] Alena Papayanis has written – in other words, we are expected [uncomplainingly] to 'make the best of things'. Contemporary reports suggest this is still very much the case in the 2020s [Pragya Agarwal gives the example of the backlash faced by Nazanin Zaghari-Ratcliffe for apparently not showing enough 'gratitude' on her release from six years' imprisonment for a crime she didn't commit].[3] I imagine, though, that for women in the UK of my grandmothers' generation, a requirement to unflinchingly endure hardship and injustice – albeit of a much less horrific nature than that experienced by Zagahri-Ratcliffe – would nonetheless have been even more firmly ingrained, handed on like housework tasks and parenting techniques as part of the received wisdom of what it meant to be female. Born in the 1910s and – like so many other women of the era – having managed home, family and work together with negotiating the trauma and uncertainty of living through the Second World War, Anne Armitage and Olive Moore were experts in [mute] stoicism, an unacknowledged selflessness which continued until their deaths. In lives time and again upturned, stalled, ruptured by exclusion and absence, chronic illness and premature bereavement, we might consider that the same domestic objects capable of channelling societal judgment and stealthy control could, paradoxically, also function as workaday anchors, providing their own humble affirmation of selves too long unarticulated, quieted by gendered convention's people-pleasing remit to *put up with*, *get on* and *make do*.

In common with many of her working class peers, Anne was eligible for a grammar school scholarship – but this was not enough to counteract prohibitive uniform and equipment costs, or the loss of wage contributions to family finances that continuing in education would bring. Denied her ambition of becoming a biochemist, instead she worked shifts at the [then] Sheffield-based dried food giant Batchelors, raised a family, and embarked on a programme of self-tutoring which took in everything from detective fiction and sci-fi to natural history and conversational Russian, courtesy of an outstanding public library system and crack-of-dawn tv broadcasts which assured the attention of either the perennially enthusiastic or the perennially insomniac [she was both]. The small but eclectic collection of her own books – mostly acquired from library sales – was crammed in no particular order onto the flimsy narrow shelves of a boxy, Utility-style bookcase: an external microcosm of possible selves lived out unobtrusively in miniature. Fortified by weapons-grade tea in a tannin scarred mug, she conducted her own silent revolution of learning from the airless kitchen-diner.[4]

For my other grandmother, Olive, the strain of single-handedly running a business, bringing up a young son and being prime carer to her elderly mother while my grandfather was away in the war manifested itself in three decades of pretty much constant ill-health from her mid-forties until her death in 1986.[5] Having existed for years on tea, cigarettes and nervous energy, she was more or less confined indoors towards the end of her life. As a result, rituals centred around household items took on what in retrospect feels an almost sacred quality which, to my childhood self, felt at best comically quirky and at worst boringly over-fastidious. Replaying events through the illuminating long lenses of age and hindsight, however, I have come to appreciate that the apparent obsessions, the [to me] inexplicable house-proudness probably was not so much about how others might see Olive's house but rather more about how she saw herself. Seemingly small things such as maintaining the routine of sliced white sandwiches in the front room on Sundays, annual Boxing Day roasts and buffet suppers around a fully-extended dining table and keeping the spare bedroom spick and span, its heavy bedspread turned down and crease-free, take on a deeper significance when viewed as the caretaking of precious relics, the manageable remnants of a life previously dedicated to hosting and entertaining. To give up on the weekend teas, to permanently fold down the table, to stop twitching at the unslept-in bedcovers would have meant finally accepting that the self which thrived on what these behaviours had come to represent had been silenced for good.

Anne and Olive may not have been afforded the opportunity, may not have felt able, may not even have thought about breaking their silence, speaking loudly and openly about not just the things that had gone right but the things that had gone wrong, had hurt them or those whom they loved, had left them feeling overlooked or unfulfilled. But through Anne's bookshelves, through Olive's bread, bedding and dining table, I think both were able to do more than simply and silently 'make the best of things'. It seems to me that these everyday objects, while insignificant to others, offered – perhaps even unrealised by the women themselves – a means to move beyond the narrow horizons imposed by class bias or illness, missed opportunities or unrecognised achievements. And so among the unspoken *putting up* and *making do* to find undiscovered lost selves.

[re110324] BRIDGING

Spring 2020. Casting around for ideas for a new project, I remembered an envelope full of old family documents which had, some years earlier, been destined for the shredder, and for which I had pleaded a stay of execution. Despite the most honourable of intentions to 'do something' with these fragile, waxy fragments, they had remained silent, unread in a drawerful of similarly liminal relics – deemed too significant to throw out but for which there wasn't quite the will to archive in any meaningful way. And so there they sat, among the wedding cards, baby shoes, a relationship documented in faded 7"x5" glossy prints – the only difference being that their [by this time] customary oblivion was now lived out inside a *functional* IKEA repository instead of a *rustic* John Lewis one.

I'm not sure whether the impetus for what followed originated in a rekindled interest in the physical objects themselves, or if it was two works which got me thinking seriously about challenging archival norms and creating alternative means of documentation – Maggie Nelson's *The Argonauts* and Peter Riley's *Excavations* – that prompted me to retrieve the papers from their manila-encased limbo. Thumbing through the birth, death and marriage certificates, the deeds of burial and the last wills and testaments which mainly related to female members of my family, they soon revealed themselves as saying far more about the fathers and husbands of the women they purported to document than about their supposed subjects. This 'undocumenting' was to become the focus of a pamphlet of poetry, *M(P)atriarchive*[1]: but while writing the poems I had also read Jacques Derrida's 'Archive Fever' and I knew a bit of the 'need for archives' he interrogates was still worrying at me, restless, unresolved long after the collection had made its way into the world. Most specifically an unwillingness to let go of a sense that if people, or aspects of social history are underrepresented, misrepresented, or overlooked by official means of recording, then we should seek out other ways to redress the balance. It was out of the chattering, unsilenceable earworm of this unfinished business with the archive, bolstered by inspiration again from Nelson, along with works by Anne Carson, Susan Howe, Claudia Rankine and Jeff Hilson – which for me joined the dots between archival practices via a diverse archive of intertextual references to identity – that the poems which became *reference ≠ endorsement* emerged.

Reading Nelson's *Jane: A Murder*, Carson's *Nox*, Howe's *That This*, Rankine's *Citizen* and *Just Us* and Hilson's *Latanoprost Variations* and *Organ Music*, I was struck time and again by their unrelenting pushing of the boundaries of documentation, the agitating for a questioning of the validity of archival convention in these collections. I was drawn in particular to the way that, if we adopt an expansive definition of the term, each author 'plays the archive at its own game', producing a new record which challenges masculinist, structurally racist or elitist norms by means of the very language and practices they seek to critique. I wanted to replicate the idea of an alternative archive, but one that was built around the most mundane, quotidian items I could think of [Gertrude Stein's *Tender Buttons* also being of huge influence here] with which anyone – however officially documented or not they might have been – could have come into contact, and which bore the imprint, the significance of that contact [however well hidden] in some way. Like these authors, I also wanted to explore the possibilities of intertextual sources in achieving this recording and – inspired by Hilson in particular – most especially those whose humble unremarkableness would reflect the commonplace household items they helped to catalogue.

The domestic objects in the poems – bread, candles, bookshelves, plates, bedding, a dining table – hide in plain sight within our daily lives, ever-present yet unobtrusive, potent yet sometimes seemingly almost apologetic. Our relationship with them might, perhaps, enhance or suppress our or others' sense of our own self or their selves; signify belonging or unbelonging and societal pressures to conform; help us to deal with illness and grief or become a means of liberation or control. But where the written language of bureaucratic recording fails, where its protocols inadvertently skim over or deliberately ignore, there exists, scattered among the breadcrumbs and wax drips, ingrained in the polished wood, tucked between neatly stacked china and folded linen an archive of the everyday, classified not with formal categories and terminologies but with chips and stains, snatches of songs, instructions for use and advertising slogans. It is nothing yet everything: an unwritten testimony of things done, seen and heard, of lives lived which tells us as much as – maybe more than – 'official' deeds and documentations ever could.[2]

REFERENCES AND WORKS CITED

[re 201023] I WANNA BE LIKE YOU?

[1] Kelly-Ann Allen, 'The Science Behind Our Need to Belong', *Psychology Today*, 3 February 2022 https://www.psychologytoday.com/us/blog/sense-belonging/202202/the-science-behind-our-need-belong [accessed 19 October 2023].

[2] Allen, 'The Science Behind Our Need to Belong'.

[3] Jenn Granneman, 'Are You an Introvert, a Highly Sensitive Person, or Both?', *Psychology Today*, 23 February 2023 https://www.psychologytoday.com/gb/blog/the-secret-lives-of-introverts/202302/are-you-an-introvert-a-highly-sensitive-person-or-both [accessed 19 October 2023].

[4] Carol Bainbridge, 'Introvert Social Needs and Preferences', *Verywell Family*, 22 February 2021 https://www.verywellfamily.com/all-about-introverts-1449354 [accessed 20 October 2023].

[5] Garo Kotchounian, 'Introverts don't like attention. Even lie to steer away eyeballs.', *Successful Introverts' Club*, 13 July 2022 https://successfulintroverts.club/introverts-dont-like-attention-even-lie-to-steer-away-eyeballs/ [accessed 20 October 2023].

[6] Jim Duffy, 'Why lockdown is heaven for introverts like me', Scotsman (30 October 2020) https://www.scotsman.com/news/opinion/columnists/why-lockdown-heaven-introverts-me-jim-duffy-3019045 [accessed 1 May 2022].

[re240223] 'NO HOPE IN DAINTINESS AND DETERMINATION'

[1] Gertrude Stein, 'ROASTBEEF' in *Tender Buttons*, Project Gutenberg ebook https://www.gutenberg.org/ebooks/15396 [accessed 30 October 2023].

[2] Ann Oakley, The Sociology of Housework, (Oxford, Cambridge MA: Blackwell, 1985), p. 2.

[3] Oakley, pp. 87- 88.

[4] Ibid., p. 92.

[5] Ibid., pp. 54, 121.

[6] 'A virgin a whole virgin is judged' - Stein, 'IN BETWEEN', *Tender Buttons*.

[7] 'A suitable establishment, well housed, practical, patient and staring, a suitable bedding, very suitable and not more particularly than complaining, anything suitable is so necessary.' - Stein, 'A CHAIR', *Tender Buttons*.

[8] For more information, see: Jean Duncombe and Dennis Marsden, 'Love and Intimacy: The Gender Division of Emotion and `Emotion Work'', *Sociology*, 27.2 (May 1993), 221-241 https://doi.org/10.1177/0038038593027002003.

Jean Duncombe and Dennis Marsden, "Workaholics' and 'Whingeing Women': Theorising Intimacy and Emotion Work — The Last Frontier of Gender Inequality?', *The Sociological Review*, 43.1 (February 1995), 150-169 https://doi.org/10.1111/j.1467-954X.1995.tb02482.x.

[9] BBC, 'Women still do more household chores than men, ONS finds', *BBC*, 10 November 2016 https://www.bbc.com/news/uk-37941191 [accessed 6 February 2023].

[10] What the position was in homes which do not conform to heteronormative notions of the family unit is not clear from the articles quoted.

[11] Dan Ascher, 'Coronavirus: 'Mums do most childcare and chores in lockdown'', *BBC*, 27 May 2020 https://www.bbc.co.uk/news/business-52808930 [accessed 8 February 2023].

[re240423] **TRIPLE LETTERED ACCEPTANCE**

[1] Eryc Eyl, 'TLAs are a PITA: Why you should stop using acronyms', *LinkedIn*, (29 September 2014) TLAs are a PITA: Why you should stop using acronyms (linkedin.com) [accessed 7 February 2023].

[re240423] **FOLLOWING THE RULE**

[1] 'a collection of three words, phrases, sentences, lines, paragraphs/stanzas, chapters/sections of writing and even whole books. The three elements together are known as a triad' - Wikipedia, 'Rule of three (writing), *Wikipedia* https://en.wikipedia.org/w/index.php?title=Rule_of_three_(writing)&oldid=1181794642 [accessed 26 October 2023].

[2] 'Hendiatris (Greek for "one through three") is a figure of speech used for emphasis, in which three words are used to express one idea'. - 'Hendiatris', *Academic Dictionaries and Encyclopedias* https://en-academic.com/dic.nsf/enwiki/784224 [accessed 27 October 2023].

[3] 'a rhetorical term that consists of three parallel clauses, phrases, or words, which happen to come in quick succession without any interruption'. - 'Tricolon', *EnglishLiterature.Net* https://englishliterature.net/literary-devices/tricolon [accessed 26 October 2023].

[4] I am indebted to Jeff Hilson's essay 'Why I Wrote *Stretchers*' in *Stretchers* (Hastings: Reality Street Editions, 2006), pp. 69-75 for prompting me to consider my own use of form.

[5] Jan Fields, 'Introduction to the Rule of Three', *Institute For Writers* (8 June 2023) https://www.instituteforwriters.com/introduction-to-the-rule-of-three/ [accessed 26 October 2023].

[6] Robert C Barkman [referencing Neil deGrasse Tyson], 'Why the Human Brain Is So Good at Detecting Patterns', *Psychology Today* (19 May 2021) https://www.psychologytoday.com/gb/blog/singular-perspective/202105/why-the-human-brain-is-so-good-detecting-patterns [accessed 30 October 2023].

[7] Jan Fields, 'Introduction to the Rule of Three'.

[8] 'In marketing theory, American advertising pioneer, E. St. Elmo Lewis laid out his three chief copywriting principles, which he felt were crucial for effective advertising: ...to attract... to interest... to convince...'- Rule of three, 'What Is The Mysterious Rule Of Three', *rule of three* https://www.rule-of-three.co.uk/articles/what-is-the-rule-of-three-copywriting [accessed 26 October 2023].

[9] Tess Jaray, *Tess Jaray: Paintings and Drawings Across 60 Years*, 20 July – 13 October 2024, Millennium Gallery, Sheffield.

[re181023] **KEEPING UP WITH THE JONESES?**

[1] Merriam Webster 'keep up with the joneses idiom', *Merriam Webster*, https://www.merriam-webster.com/dictionary/keep+up+with+the+Joneses [accessed 17 October 2023].

[2] 'Material goods act as symbolic representations of the images consumers have of themselves that they want to express to surrounding others. Material goods can also signify group membership'. - Ronald Earl Goldsmith and Ronald A Clark, 'Materialism, Status Consumption, and Consumer Independence', *The Journal of Social Psychology*, 152.1 (January 2012), 43-60 (p. 44) https://doi.org/10.1080/00224545.2011.555434.

[3] Born approximately 1965-1984. - Wikipedia, 'Generation X', *Wikipedia* https://en.wikipedia.org/w/index.php?title=Generation_X&oldid=1180464712 [accessed 17 October 2023].

[4] Character in BBC TV's *The Good Life* by John Esmonde and Bob Larbey (aired 1975-1978).

[5] Character in BBC TV's *Keeping Up Appearances* by Roy Clarke (aired 1990-1995).

[6] Charlotte McDougall, 'We've all met a Margo': Penelope Keith's comic triumph on The Good Life', *Guardian* (8 July 2015) https://www.theguardian.com/stage/2015/jul/08/charlotte-mcdougall-on-penelope-keith-margo-good-life-comedy-hero [accessed 3 November 2023].

[7] Born approximately 1946-1964. - Wikipedia, 'Baby Boomers', *Wikipedia* https://en.wikipedia.org/w/index.php?title=Baby_boomers&oldid=1176141078 [accessed 18 October 2023].

[8] Rebecca Leach, Simon Biggs, Chris Phillipson and Annemarie Money, 'Boomers and Beyond: intergenerational consumption and the mature imagination', *Cultures of Consumption* project 2005-2007 http://www.consume.bbk.ac.uk/research/biggs.html [accessed 17 October2023].

[9] Stephanie Linning, 'Argos catalogues reveal biggest kitchen trends of the last 50 years', *Daily Mail* (19 June 2018) http://www.dailymail.co.uk/femail/article-5856905/Retro-Argos-catalogues-reveal-biggest-kitchen-trends-50-years.html [accessed 27 December 2022].

[10] D. Jasun Carr, Melissa R. Gotlieb, Nam-Jin Lee and Dhavan V. Shah, 'Examining Overconsumption, Competitive Consumption, and Conscious Consumption from 1994 to 2004: Disentangling Cohort and Period Effects', *The Annals of the American Academy of Political and Social Science* 644.1 (November 2012), 220-233 (p. 221) https://doi.org/10.1177/0002716212449452.

[11] There is a whole other piece to be written on the over-use/misuse of this word.

[12] BBC TV series (originally aired 1996-2004, revived by Channel 4 2021-2022).

[13] Carr et al [quoting Juliet Schor], p. 221.

[14] McDougall, 'We've all met a Margo': Penelope Keith's comic triumph on The Good Life'.

[re241023] *WHY WINNICOTT NOW*

[1] 'One of this book's titles, in an alternate universe' - Maggie Nelson, *The Argonauts* (London: Melville House UK, 2016), p. 23.

[2] Robert Adès, 'Winnicott: the 'good-enough mother' radio broadcasts', *OUPblog* (1 December 2016) https://blog.oup.com/2016/12/winnicott-radio-broadcasts/ [accessed 24 October 2023].

[3] D W Winnicott, *Playing and Reality* (London: Pelican, 1988), p. 166.

[4] Adès, 'Winnicott: the 'good-enough mother' radio broadcasts'.

[5] Ibid.

[6] Patient, 'How to cope with the stress of being a new parent', *Patient* (24 November 2021, updated by Lydia Smith 3 March 2023) https://patient.info/news-and-features/how-to-cope-with-the-stress-of-being-a-new-parent [accessed 21 July 2023].

[7] Stokke, 'Research on the challenge of bringing home a new baby', *LinkedIn* (8 November 2021) https://www.linkedin.com/pulse/stokke-research-challenge-bringing-home-new-baby-stokke/?trk=organization-update-content_share-article [accessed 24 October 2023].

[8] Adès, 'Winnicott: the 'good-enough mother' radio broadcasts'.

[9] Nelson, *The Argonauts*, p. 118.

[re050324] MAKING THE BEST OF IT

[1] A version of this essay was presented as a conference paper *Why Is A Line Of Washing A 'Nice' Sight?': Household Objects, Ritual And Documentation*, 'Transcendence and the Sacred' (31 May 2024), University of Sheffield, University of Sheffield School of English Postgraduate Colloquium https://www.pgrcolloquiumsheffield2024.co.uk/programme.

[2] Alena Papayanis, 'Women Are Taught To Be Nice. Here's What Happened When I Stopped.', *HuffPost*, 7 January 2022 https://www.huffpost.com/entry/women-socialized-to-be-nice_n_61d7612be4b04b42ab7d7196 [accessed 5 March 2024].

[3] Pragya Agarwal, 'Why are women always expected to be grateful?', *Harper's Bazaar*, 6 April 2022 https://www.harpersbazaar.com/uk/culture/a39649521/women-expected-gratitude/ [accessed 5 March 2024]. It should also be noted that Agarwal observes the enhanced level of expectation on women of colour.

[4] Elements of this paragraph first appeared in A J Moore, 'Three Poems About Absence: A Creative Response To Women's History Month'.

[5] This is explored in more detail in my pamphlet *M(P)atriarchive*, (Tipperary: Beir Bua Press, 2021).

[re110324] BRIDGING

[1] Beir Bua Press, 2021. Elements of this paragraph were first mentioned in my 'Introduction' to the pamphlet.

[2] Elements of this paragraph have appeared in my article: A J Moore, 'Three Poems About Absence: A Creative Response To Women's History Month'.

Notes on intertextual sources

GEN/HHOLD/FOOD/1/BREAD

[br011221] **staff of life**

'"Bread", says he, "dear brothers is the staff of life"', Jonathan Swift, *A Tale of a Tub*.

[br151221] **breaking bread**

wishful sinful – title of the 1969 single by The Doors, written by Robby Krieger.

non-standardised south east – term used by Rebecca Hardy in a *Guardian* article exploring presumptions about northern accents (*I've got a northern accent but I'm not working class. So what am I?*, 23 May 2016)

[br211221] **rising?**

there for you's – fragment of title of The Rembrandts' 1995 hit 'I'll Be There For You', theme song of the pervasive and prodigiously popular US sitcom *Friends*, written by Michael Skloff and Allee Willis.

[br040122] **all sorrows are less**

'All sorrows are less with bread', Miguel de Cervantes, *Don Quixote*.

GEN/HHOLD/MISC/2/CANDLES

[c090322] **light of the world**

This is the sound – Text spoken by actor Patrick Allen over the opening of Frankie Goes To Hollywood's 1984 hit *Two Tribes*, taken from Allen's voiceover for the *Protect and Survive* public information films.

not walking in darkness – 'I am the light of the world. Whoever follows me will not walk in darkness, but will have the light of life' (John 8:12).

[c080723] **to cast a shadow**

'To light a candle is to cast a shadow', Ursula K. Le Guin, *A Wizard of Earthsea*.

Love me say you do – lyric fragment from the song *Wild is the Wind*, theme to the 1957 film, written by Dimitri Tiomkin and Ned Washington and covered by David Bowie on his 1976 album *Station to Station*.

[c040422] **put out the light**

'Put out the light, and then put out the light' (William Shakespeare, *Othello*: Act V Scene II line vii).

[c080422] **brief candles**

'Out, out, brief candle' (William Shakespeare, *Macbeth*: Act V Scene IV line xxiii).

GEN/HHOLD/FURN/3/BOOKSHELVES

[bk210722] **hers for the reading**

'The world was hers for the reading.' Betty Smith, *A Tree Grows in Brooklyn*.

[bk200722] **primary sources**

ripping times – 'Me and my cloak and fangs/Had ripping times in the dark', Philip Larkin, 'A Study Of Reading Habits'.

shaken not stirred – Ian Fleming's much-quoted description (actually 'shaken and not stirred') of James Bond's martini requirements, first used in *Diamonds Are Forever*.

[bk290822] **renewing**

second time around – *The Second Time Around*, 1960 song by Sammy Cahn and Jimmy Van Heusen, popularised by Frank Sinatra.

[bk050922] **remote access**

too little too late too flawed – 'UK's response to Covid-19 "too little, too late, too flawed"', *BMJ*, 15 May 2020.

hungered for touch – lyric fragment from 'Unchained Melody' (1955) written by Alex North and Hy Zaret.

GEN/HHOLD/CRCK/4/PLATES

[p211222] **what they've always wanted**

measured out – 'I have measured out my life with coffee spoons', T. S. Eliot, 'The Love Song of J. Alfred Prufrock'.

[p120123] **crazed**

licence revoked – original title of the sixteenth James Bond film which eventually became *Licence to Kill*.

GEN/HHOLD/LNNS/5/BEDDING

[be210723] **safe in their beds**

'We sleep safe in our beds because rough men stand ready in the night to visit violence on those who would do us harm.' George Orwell.

GEN/HHOLD/FURN/6/DINING TABLE

[dt180124] **sapling**

just begun's – lyric fragment from The Carpenters' 1970 hit 'We've Only Just Begun', written by Paul Williams and Roger Nichols.

[dt120224] **veteran**

slow dying – 'Life is slow dying', Philip Larkin, 'Nothing To Be Said'.

The poems in this collection also feature fragments of found language discovered lurking in various online locations – from interior design websites to medical equipment retailers to arboriculture specialists – too numerous to mention individually here. Broadly, these include [but are not limited to] YouTube, Pinterest, eBay, Amazon, vintage and contemporary advertisements, instruction manuals, catalogues of various kinds, Sunday supplement articles and digital library systems. I am grateful to all these [and other] sources for helping me to find inspiration in the everyday.

Acknowledgements

A huge debt of gratitude is owed to Dr Ágnes Lehóczky and Professor Adam Piette, for their valuable advice, infinite supply of inspirational reading suggestions, unstinting support and patience, and for providing a platform for some of the poems to be read at The University of Sheffield Centre for Poetry, Poetics and Creative Writing. My thanks also to Dr Jonathan Ellis for additional support and cups of coffee!

Sincere thanks to the following, who have all read and commented on various sections, for their insights, observations and support: Helen Angell, Heather Beier, Jan Ellen, Lydia Lord, Ethel Maqeda, Leonie Martin, Meg Meredith, Jo Mincher, Suzanne Reynolds, Ella Ruby Self, Julia South, Alan Wade, Llew Watkins, Amber Whitham.

Extra special thanks to Mark Lindsey for reading every section (often more than once!), for wise words and always excellent suggestions.

Thank you to Mark Leigh and Oskar Leigh for believing in the project and giving me the space to do this. Their support and encouragement has been invaluable.

Earlier versions of some of the poems appeared in the following: *Objects* (Dunlin Press), *eYeland* #3 (c22 Press), *Twisted Ink* 1, *D.O.R.* 1 (LJMcD Communications), *The Sheffield Review* (formerly *Route 57*), The University of Sheffield Faculty of Arts International Women's Day Project 2023. I am hugely grateful to all of the editors for accepting my work.

Special thanks to Ansgar Allen at Erratum Press for giving the work a home.

A J MOORE has published work in *Twisted Ink*, *Objects* (Dunlin Press), *The Sheffield Review/Route 57*, *Blackbox Manifold*, *D.O.R*, *eYeland*, *For The Love Of*, *The Babel Tower Noticeboard*, *Beir Bua Journal*, and is the author of the chapbooks *M(P)atriarchive* (Beir Bua Press) and *Zeitgeist* (c22 Press). She is a founder member of Cut Collective Writers: cutcollectivewriters.org

Praise for *Reference ≠ Endorsement*

"In a world where we're conditioned to seek neat narratives, *Reference ≠ Endorsement* delivers a necessary and visceral rupture. This collection of prose poems operates like a post-Benjaminian archive, meticulously shredding, dismantling, and reassembling the detritus of domestic life, memory, and the female body. Its syntax is physically broken, almost obsessive in its precision, creating suffocating, dizzying spacetime vacuums that spiral inward and outward—part exhibition, part confession, part cell.

Drawing from fragments of language found lurking in the digital ether—from interior design sites to medical equipment retailers—and focusing on the potent, often apologetic presence of everyday objects like bread, candles, and dining tables, this work explores how our most intimate possessions can signify belonging, unbelonging, and even act as means of liberation or control.

With the brutal, steel-toned language of conceptual poetics tempered by intimate, factual essays, *Reference ≠ Endorsement* approaches what can only be described as a feminized machinery of thought—at once clinical yet intuitive, factual yet profoundly wounded. Here, womanhood are not merely lived but practised, unpractised, prescribed, and undone, rebuilt from fragments of suffering and archival dust. This is a mesmerising archival project that explores what is left behind when presence is removed, what accumulates in the silent folds of fabric, and what survives inside syntactic units that resemble prisons more than sentences.

A relentless and terrifyingly precise book, *Reference ≠ Endorsement* doesn't seek lyricism but instead finds a devastating intimacy in the mechanics of ruin. It's a wonderful collection designed to haunt, clink, and reverberate long after you turn the final page."

—Ágnes Lehóczky

"*Reference ≠ Endorsement* is an incisive, rich, poetic, intertextual scrutinising of the culture, history and politics behind the objects that quietly and sometimes sinisterly shape our lives. A J Moore's playful linguistic experiments cut through layers of nostalgic myth and comfortable complacency to deconstruct such seeming innocuous objects as bread, candles, dinner plates and book shelves, both illuminating and as often satirising the powerful forces that encourage the consumption, conservatism and competitiveness that go into designing the domestic. *Reference ≠ Endorsement* once again confirms A J Moore as among my favourite poets."

—Mark Lindsey

"*Reference ≠ Endorsement* reframes domestic space through an intimate anti-archive of objects. Family history, feminist theory, and practice are intertextually intermingled with refreshing formal ingenuity in this collection as commentary on its own making is folded into the body of the poetic text."

—JR Carpenter

"A J Moore decrypts the signs and inscriptions of a hoard of forms, birth-, marriage-, death-certificates, letters, photographs, tracking the ways lives and bodies are subject to bureaucratized surveillance, biopowerful scripting, regulated governmentality of the matter of our kin. The prose poems rummage through the cardboard boxes of the family archive as though also acting as a bureau shaping the data doubles of the maternal and the paternal lines and lives, but also enact oblique and moving forms of elegy and recuperation. This is astonishing work, manifesting as a compelling and eloquent challenge to the archive in its miming of the regulator's erasures, censorships and rationalities that brings difficult sympathies to bear upon these Sheffield working-class lives across the 19th and 20th century, in sickness and in health, in war and peace, through life and death, as family history and trace under the eyes of power."

—Adam Piette

PREVIOUSLY PUBLISHED AT ERRATUM PRESS

Aussi/Or
Toby Fitch

the poems
William Walsh

Hermeslang
Spyridon St. Kogkas

the absurd fade
Michael Mc Aloran

Traumnovelle
Grant Maierhofer

Zipf Maneuvers
Andrew C. Wenaus & Germán Sierra

Homo Catastrophicus
Louis Armand

Warewolff!
Gary J. Shipley

Today Yesterday After My Death
Maureen Alsop

Last Days of Pompeii: A Comedy Vols.1 & 2
Steve Hanson

retrocede
Michael Mc Aloran

LRD
Grant Maierhofer

The Poets
William Walsh

The Chief of Birds
Michael Templeton

Lord of Chaos
Daniel Beauregard

If I Had Not Seen Their Sleeping Faces
Christina Tudor-Sideri

The Prodigious Earth
Eric Blix

Morant
Roy Goddard

bone bite snare
Michael Mc Aloran

The Face Hole
Gary J. Shipley

Dreams of Amputation
Gary J. Shipley

The Scourge of Villanie
John Marston

Civilisation: Its Cause and Cure
Edward Carpenter

www.ingramcontent.com/pod-product-compliance
Lightning Source LLC
Chambersburg PA
CBHW060500080526
44584CB00015B/1491